MELANNIE SVOBODA, SND

Just because

PRAYER-POEMS TO DELIGHT THE HEART

Sr. Melannie Svoboda, SND

TWENTY THIRD *23rd*
PUBLICATIONS
www.23rdpublications.com

DEDICATION

To Bishop Robert F. Morneau
...just because

TWENTY-THIRD PUBLICATIONS
A Division of Bayard
One Montauk Avenue, Suite 200
New London, CT 06320
(860) 437-3012 or (800) 321-0411
www.23rdpublications.com

The Scripture passages contained herein are from the *New Revised Standard Version of the Bible*, copyright ©1989, by the Division of Christian Education of the National Council of Churches in the U.S.A. All rights reserved.

Cover image: ©iStockphoto.com/canismajor

ISBN 978-1-58595-774-3
Library of Congress Catalog Card Number: 2010920815
Printed in the U.S.A.

CONTENTS

INTRODUCTION

*P*oetry is a lot like prayer. Prayer is a lot like poetry. First, they both arise from a deep attentiveness to life—whether to a rose, a grain of sand, a baby's laugh, a particular hurt, an interior joy or dread. Both poetry and prayer tend to displace the logical and rational in favor of metaphor and feeling. They both have the uncanny ability to put us into the presence of the universal and eternal, thus connecting us with others, with nature, and with the entire world. "All poetry is prayer," said Samuel Beckett the Irish novelist, dramatist, and poet. Perhaps we could also say, "All prayer is poetry."

This book is for people who like poetry as well as for those who shy away from it. It is for those who like to pray and those who know the struggle of prayer. All the poems in these pages invite you to prayer. They are simple, varied in form, and diverse in content and theme. There are, for example, poems on prayer, friendship, love, hatred, war, fear, hope, change, grief, and death. Other poems focus on specific incidents—wearing a mother's apron, ending a relationship. Still others are rooted in sacred Scripture—the parable of the Good Samaritan, the wedding feast at Cana, the woman at the well. You can simply enjoy and ponder these poems in their own right.

But there is more here than poems. After each is a brief commentary that tells how the poem came to be or offers a few thoughts about its theme, content, or structure. Next come reflection questions for personal pondering and group sharing. These questions are followed

1

by suggested Scripture passages that relate to the poem in some way. And finally, there is an activity or two for prayer and play. (Just as poetry and prayer are a lot alike, so too are prayer and play.)

These prayer poems are arranged alphabetically according to their titles. In order to make the book more helpful, there is an index of all the referred-to Scripture passages, as well as an index on the subjects and themes. In this way, if you need a poem or prayer for a certain Scripture passage or a particular occasion, these may help you to find something appropriate.

I have titled this little book *Just Because* since for me this phrase suggests something that can't be captured in words. We love a certain friend "just because." We cannot explain why, for in the end all love is beyond comprehension and articulation. My hope is that these prayer poems, in some small way, will help you to grow in knowledge and love of God who ultimately loves us just because.

Annunciations

The truth is,
God does show up,
often when we least expect it:
while tending sheep,
threshing wheat,
working at our desk,
peeling potatoes,
puttering in the garden,
walking the dog.
God comes,
(or barges in or sneaks up on.)
And we're allowed
to be surprised, taken aback,
frightened, incredulous.
Then God invites.
And it's perfectly understandable
if we're puzzled or disturbed.
And, yes, we're allowed

to ask questions,
to offer excuses,
to bewail, "Why me?"
or protest, "I can't!"
But eventually,
eventually,
eventually,
we learn to bow our head,
and pronounce our yes
whether willingly or
begrudgingly.
Then God leaves,
(not really, of course.)
And all may look the same
as before,
but no, no,
everything is changed—
everything.

*W*hen we hear the word "annunciation," we often think of the angel Gabriel's visit to Mary. But there are many other Annunciations in Scripture—for example, Moses and the burning bush, the call of Gideon, the vision of Zachariah, and even St. Joseph and his dream. As diverse as these annunciations are, the basic pattern, as this poem illustrates, is essentially the same.

FOR REFLECTION

1. How does this poem illustrate both the diversity and the similarity of these various annunciations? Why do you think the word "eventually" is repeated three times?

2. How has God "shown up" in your life? Reflect on a particular "annunciation" you have experienced.

Suggested Scripture

Luke 2:26–38 *Mary's Annunciation*

Exodus 3:1—4:1–17 *Moses and the burning bush*

Judges 6:11–24 *The call of Gideon*

Matthew 1:18–25 *St. Joseph's dream*

FOR PRAYER AND PLAY

Mary was not forced to say "yes" to God's invitation to be the mother of Jesus. Come up with four or five good excuses she could have used for declining God's request. Or reflect on two or more of the annunciations above. How are they different from each other? How are they the same?

Baggage Claim

I envy travelers
who deplane
with only a duffle bag
slung over their shoulder,
and march out the door
and into their waiting cars.
While I
follow the throng
all the way down
to baggage claim,
where I stand and wait,
and stand and wait
for the conveyer belt
to squawk its alarm
and begin to go
around and around.

There is this rule:
the first bags through
never belong to me

or to anyone else standing there.
Instead, like orphans on a
carrousel,
they ride around
a dozen times
before my bags appear.

As I pull off my first bag
and wait for the second,
I vow to never again
pack so much stuff,
assuring myself
I need far less
for my happiness
while away from home.
But I know:
next time I pack
I'll toss in this
and tuck in that
just in case.

I travel a lot, so I'm always packing and unpacking suitcases. Whenever I fly, I am amazed at the diversity of suitcases I see among my fellow travelers. Some bags are small and discreet, others huge and bulging. Even when I lift my own suitcase and feel its heftiness, I'll ask myself, "What did you put in here anyway?" It's as if I can't believe the number the things I deemed were essential for this particular trip. This poem, however, is not simply about baggage. It's about all the "stuff" we think we have to have as we travel through life.

FOR REFLECTION

1. When you travel, what is your attitude toward packing suitcases? Do you find it fun, difficult, burdensome? Why?

2. On a deeper level, how are you traveling through life—lightly or with a lot of "stuff"?

Suggested Scripture

Matthew 16:24–28 *conditions for discipleship*

Mark 6:6–13 *the mission of the twelve*

Luke 12:16–21 *parable of the rich fool*

Luke 18:18–30 *the rich official*

FOR PRAYER AND PLAY

Read the Scripture passages above. What insights do they offer about "traveling light"? Or if you had to evacuate your house and could take only five items with you (excluding people and pets!), what would you take and why? Or go through your closets and drawers. What items can you donate to others?

❦ 3 ❧

Barney the Beagle

Barney the beagle scurries through the park,
his snout glued to the ground.
Like a frantic vacuum cleaner,
he sucks up every scent he comes upon.
(Urine and poop
excite him the most, I notice.)
Smells are his morning newspaper,
crammed with information
only he can decipher and savor,
while I, securely leashed,
and straining along behind him,
sniff the air repeatedly
in quest of a whiff
of anything.

*W*e had a beagle when I was a little girl growing up on our farm. I was amazed at how he always kept his nose stuck to the ground wherever he went. "He looks like a vacuum cleaner," my mother once remarked. Later I came to realize just how powerful a dog's nose is—especially a hound's. It's thousands of times stronger and more sensitive than the nose of us poor humans. This poem illustrates that contrast.

FOR REFLECTION

1. What has been your experience with dogs? Is it essentially positive or negative?

2. Who is "securely leashed" in this poem? Barney, his owner, or both?

Suggested Scripture

Psalm 36   *divine providence*

Luke 16:19–31   *story of the rich man and Lazarus*

FOR PRAYER AND PLAY

What scents or smells do you like the most? List a few of them and reflect on how they make you feel? Or, be especially attentive to everything you smell today—for example, soap, flowers, food, candles. Notice the effect each of these scents has on you.

The Barren Cross Blossomed

The barren cross blossomed,
the legend says,
after he was laid to rest.
The dead wood
put out tendrils at first
and then a cascade
of white flowers—
or were they red?

Their color is irrelevant,
so too their kind.
Even whether
the whole thing
really happened
or not
is beside the point.

What matters most
is the story's truth:
from ugliness, agony, death
exquisite beauty
can take root.

*W*hen I would read a short story with my students, they would often ask me, "Is it true?" What they usually meant was, "Did it actually happen?" I would painstakingly try to lead them to see that there are other kinds of truth besides the mere factual or historical. It's easy to dismiss a story or, in this case, a legend as not being true. But if we do that, we risk missing the deeper truth the legend sets before us.

FOR REFLECTION

1. What examples of beauty "took root" in the crucifixion of Jesus? Have you ever experienced or witnessed beauty being born from ugliness, agony, or death?

2. What other legends or stories can you think of that present an important truth?

Suggested Scripture

Luke 15:11–32 *parable of the prodigal son*

Luke 24:13–35 *the appearance of Jesus on the road to Emmaus*

FOR PRAYER AND PLAY

After reading Jesus' parable of the prodigal son, reflect on these questions: Where is the pain and ugliness in the story? Where is the beauty? Or, read the account of Jesus' appearance to the two disciples on the road to Emmaus. Where is the pain? Where is the joy?

Children of the Exodus

We were children of the Exodus,
Witness to the Breading.
We danced in Breadflakes
from the sky
And even went Bread sledding.

We fashioned Breadballs
with our hands
And tossed them at each other
While gathering up and
giving thanks
Were our father and our mother.

In the evening the
Bread was gone,
But we went to bed well fed.

We had no fear,
knowing God was near,
And with the dawn, more Bread.

We're grownups of the
Promised Land,
The bread we eat we make.
We have arrived;
our children eat
Cookies, sweets, and cake.

But after meals we hunger still.
Though what we eat
should satisfy,
We long for days of journeying
And Bread from out the sky!

*W*andering in a desert for forty years was a severe hardship for the Israelites. Yet God took care of them in their need, providing miraculous bread called "manna" in the desert to sustain them on their journey. The manna was abundant—as this poem fancifully presents. But the children of the exodus are now adults and have no need to wander or hunger again. Yet, some of them still pine for the "good old days" of wandering and hungering. This poem says something about the advantages of hardship, the blessing of need.

FOR REFLECTION

1. Have you ever experienced hardship as a blessing? When, where, how?

2. In what way can affluence and security be hindrances to real happiness?

Suggested Scripture

Exodus 16:4–36 *manna in the wilderness*

John 6:22–51 *the bread of life discourse*

FOR PRAYER AND PLAY

Bake a loaf of bread today or get a fresh loaf from a bakery. Eat one slice slowly and prayerfully: smelling it, examining its texture, putting your favorite spread on it, and savoring every single bite. Thank God for bread today. Thank God for your needs too.

Come and Slow Me Down

Come, Lord Jesus!
You who took time to notice
lilies bobbing,
birds soaring, and bread rising,
Come and slow me down.

You who took time to dine
with acquaintances,
go fishing with your apostles,
and barbecue breakfast on the
beach for your friends,
Come and slow me down.

You who took time to play
with children,
listen to people's stories,
and share their joys and sorrows,
Come and slow me down.

When my mind is stuffed
with plans,
when my "to-do" list is pages long,

when I feel carried away by
conflicting concerns,
Come and slow me down.

Give me the grace to stop
and to be—
with you,
with others,
with my own hopes, fears,
questions, and dreams.

Help me to bear you,
slowly but surely, into the world,
a world languishing and lovely,
dark and delightful,
sinful and saintly.

I ask these things of you
through Mary,
the pondering disciple,
your mother and mine.
Come, Lord Jesus, come! Amen.

*T*his poem was originally written for Advent, but it is appropriate for all seasons. Many of us live busy lives. Amid all the hectic activity, we must remember to take time to slow down, pause, reflect, enjoy, pray. We have good models in Jesus and in Mary his mother.

FOR REFLECTION

1. Are there any phrases or lines in this poem that resonate with you right now? If so, why?

2. Mary's canticle, her "magnificat," was the outgrowth of her prayerful pondering. What does it say about God? For whom is the canticle good news? For whom is it bad news?

Suggested Scripture

Luke 1:29 *Mary pondered*

Luke 1:46–56 *Mary's canticle*

Luke 2:15–20 *shepherd's visit*

Luke 2:41–52 *the boy Jesus in the temple*

FOR PRAYER AND PLAY

The other three Scripture passages show Mary pondering or reflecting on the people and events in her life. Do you ponder or reflect on the people and events in your life? If so, when and how? Or make a list of the things you do or could do to slow down when your life gets too hectic.

The Creation of the Camel

On the way to creating the horse,
God first made the camel.
As soon as God saw it,
he knew it was all wrong:
the head was too big,
the neck sagged,
and the back had a
big hump on it.
The ears were too small,
too round, and too far back
on the head.
The lower lip and nose protruded,
the coat was scraggly,
and God knew he could do
a better job on those legs.

Yet,
when God looked into
those eyes,
he smiled and said,
"Well, at least I got the
eyes right!"

That's why today
we have both camels and horses,
and not just horses.
For God is like the master potter
who—even after fashioning
elegant bowls, vases, and jars—
could not bear to discard
his first pinch pot.

*T*his whimsical account of the creation of the camel is certainly not a study in evolution. It simply celebrates God's incredible creativity and love for all of creation.

FOR REFLECTION

1. Name some aspects of God's vast creation that you find particularly fascinating or enchanting.

2. Jesus was attentive to the animals in his world. What animals in particular was he familiar with?

Suggested Scripture

Jeremiah 18:1–6 *God as the potter*

Mark 10:25 *camel and the eye of a needle*

Matthew 23:24 *swallowing a camel*

FOR PRAYER AND PLAY

Play with some modeling clay for a while, creating whatever you like. How did you feel about this experience? Or, write a prayer of thanksgiving to God for specific aspects of God's creation that mean a lot to you.

Cuteness

I learned today
that sparrows are quite vicious.
Those cute little birds,
endeared forever
by Jesus' words,
will attack and peck
a bluebird to death,
destroy her eggs,
and usurp her nest.

This knowledge, My Love,
causes me to sigh:
What ferocity
might thy cuteness belie?

*D*on't judge a book by its cover," the old proverb says. This light little poem conveys a similar serious theme found throughout literature: "Things aren't always what they seem," or "Appearances can be deceiving."

FOR REFLECTION

1. When have you experienced the truth, "Don't judge a book by its cover" or "Things aren't always what they seem"?

2. Jesus became very angry at hypocrisy. What exactly is hypocrisy and why do you think it angered Jesus so?

Suggested Scripture

Psalm 1   *happiness in following God's law*

Matthew 23:23–29   *woe to the scribes and Pharisees*

Mark 12:41–44   *the poor widow's contribution*

FOR PRAYER AND PLAY

Reflect on some ways you can guard against hypocrisy in your personal life. What are some ways you can grow in personal integrity, that is, in honesty, uprightness, and sincerity? Or read the account of the poor widow's generous contribution to the Temple treasury. Rewrite the story in contemporary times.

Deliverance

"There's a big black ant on the counter,"
I yell to him.
He strolls into the kitchen
armed with a tissue
and ever so gently picks up the ant
and deposits it outside on the lawn.
Next time it's a hairy brown spider
scowling at me from the tub.
For this one
he fashions a funnel out of newspaper,
coaxes the thing in,
and carries it outside like an Olympic torch bearer.
The little green inch worm
he slips into the envelope from our electric bill,
the squirming cricket he cups in his bare hands.
After each deliverance,
I plant a kiss on his cheek and whisper,
"My hero!"

*J*ainism is a very ancient religion in India. One of its teachings is the sacredness of all life forms. Jainists advocate harmlessness towards all, whether creatures are large or small. This policy extends even to insects. I am no Jainist, but I do have a reputation for taking bugs (ants, crickets, beetles) outside in envelopes. I've also allowed more than one small spider to cohabit in my bedroom with me.

FOR REFLECTION

1. What is your general attitude toward living things besides people—such as other animals, insects, plants? How does your behavior reflect this attitude?

2. Jesus is sometimes called "our deliverer." From what does Jesus deliver us?

Suggested Scripture

Psalm 30   *thanksgiving for deliverance*

Luke 4:16–30   *Jesus' rejection at Nazareth*

FOR PRAYER AND PLAY

Take time to observe an insect or two today. What did you learn about the insect(s) and about yourself by doing this? Or read the account of Jesus' rejection in his home town of Nazareth. Write a newspaper account of this incident for the Nazareth News & Observer.

Dote on Me Today

Almighty God,
dote on me today.
Make a funny face at me,
poke me in the ribs.
Call me sweetie,
muss up my hair.
Take me out for ice-cream.
Hang on to every word I say.

Today I need you
not as Great Jehovah,
Creator of All,
Sovereignty without end.
Today I need you
simply as
good friend.

Spiritual writers tell us our image of God is vital to our spiritual life. How we view God affects everything: our self-image, our attitude, the way we pray, the choices we make, and how we interact with others. This poem contrasts two images of God: God as the Almighty and as good friend. There are times in our lives when we probably need one more than the other.

FOR REFLECTION

1. What are some of your images of God? How did you acquire them?

2. If you related to God as good friend, what effect would that have on your self-image, attitude, prayer, choices, and the way you relate to others?

Suggested Scripture

Psalm 31:1–9 *prayer in distress*

Genesis 19:16–33 *Abraham intercedes for Sodom*

John 15:11–17 *Jesus calls his disciples friends*

FOR PRAYER AND PLAY

Read the account of Abraham interceding on behalf of the city of Sodom. Write a dialogue between yourself and God, using some of the words from this poem if you wish. Or take the word "friend." For each letter choose one word that could describe your relationship with Jesus. When you're finished, talk to Jesus about each word you chose.

The Driving Lesson

*As Adam was teaching Cain
how to drive the 4 X 4,
musing how nice it was going to be
having Cain to run to the store for Eve,
he failed to see
the glint in Cain's eye
and the smile on his lips,
as he, with one foot on the brake,
pressed down hard on the gas
and felt the incredible power
this baby had.*

*That day Cain knew:
he had one more tool
for ridding the world
of a bothersome brother—
if ever the need should arise.*

*T*he story of the first murder in Genesis is full of mystery. What caused Cain to slay his brother? Was it jealousy? Or was it something else—revenge perhaps? Was the killing premeditated or spur of the moment? And exactly how did Cain slay Abel? Scripture doesn't provide clear answers for us. We are left wondering.

FOR REFLECTION

1. Read the story of Cain and Abel. What are some of your insights into this story?

2. What are some ways we can "kill" someone without actually taking their life?

Suggested Scripture

Genesis 4:1–16 *Cain and Abel story*

1 John 3:11–18 *love for one another*

FOR PRAYER AND PLAY

Pretend you are Cain's defense attorney. What arguments would you use to minimize his sentence? Or Cain says to God, "Am I my brother's keeper?" List some of the people who have been a "keeper" for you during your life. For whom have you been a "keeper"?

ৎ 12 ৎ

Fear

Fear is a highly skilled
predator,
lurking in the shadows,
stalking in tall grass,
peering intently
for any hint of weakness in us—
a limp,
an open wound,
the slightest hesitation—
always ready to spring,
charge,
pounce,
and take us
down.

*T*he phrase "Fear not!" is one of the most often repeated admonitions in Scripture. "Fear not," God says to Abraham. "Fear Not," Moses says to the Israelites. "Fear not," the prophet Isaiah says to his people. "Fear not," the angel Gabriel says to Mary. "Fear Not," Jesus says to his disciples. The frequency of the admonition reminds us of how prevalent this particular emotion can be in our lives. It also bespeaks the danger of letting fear rule our lives.

FOR REFLECTION

1. What might the three weaknesses in this poem ("a limp, / an open wound, / the slightest hesitation") symbolize in your life?

2. What makes you afraid? What helps you to allay some of your fears?

Suggested Scripture

Psalm 56   *trust in God*

Luke 12:22–34 *dependence on God*

FOR PRAYER AND PLAY

Make a list of your fears on a sheet of paper. Talk about each one with God. Ask God to help you to trust more and worry less. Then burn, tear up, or shred your list of fears. Or write your own psalm entitled "Trust in God."

Find me, God

Find me, God.
I'm over here
in these brambles
where my wool coat
is caught and entangled.

Find me, God.
I'm over here
on the floor in the corner
where I rolled
accidentally.

Find me, God.
I'm over here
in this foreign land
where I'm cold, hungry,
afraid and alone.

Find me, God,
for I cannot find you
on my own.

*J*esus told three beautiful parables about lost things: a sheep, a coin, a son. He gave assurance that, when we are lost, all the while God (as shepherd, housewife, and father) is searching for us.

FOR REFLECTION

1. Have you ever lost something important or precious? What steps did you take to find it? If you eventually found it, how did you feel? If you never found it, how did you feel?

2. Were you ever "lost"? Were you ever "found"? If so, how did these experiences make you feel?

Suggested Scripture

Hosea 14: 2–10   *return to the Lord*

Luke 15:1–32   *three parables about lost items*

FOR PRAYER AND PLAY

Sing or listen prayerfully to the song "Amazing Grace," paying close attention to all the words. Or, make up a parable of your own about someone losing something—for example, a wallet, car keys, a pet, a journal, or an important letter.

Follow Your Thirst

If you wish to encounter Divinity,
follow your thirst.
Even the lesser ones will do at first:
more money,
companionship,
this one small success.
But don't stop there.
Keep burrowing down,
down, down,
to their roots
until you come to
that warm damp place
where love and truth
and goodness dwell.

The Samaritan woman
was simply following her thirst
to the well that day,
when she met a stranger
who drenched her
with salvation.

*T*he story of Jesus and the woman at the well is one of my favorite stories. The dialogue between the two is very real, very fresh. The woman certainly got much more than she bargained for when she made that trip to the well that day. This poem presents a positive view of our longings and desires, too, reminding us that, by following them to their roots, we are very likely to encounter Divinity.

FOR REFLECTION

1. What are some of your "lesser thirsts" right now?

2. What are three of your deepest longings?

Scripture

Psalm 42 *longing for God's presence*

John 4:4–42 *the woman at the well*

FOR PRAYER AND PLAY

Make up a tune for this verse from Psalm 42: "As the deer longs for streams of water, so my soul longs for you, O God." Sing it throughout the day. Or rewrite the dialogue between Jesus and the woman at the well in contemporary terms.

∽ 15 ∾

Here Is the Key to My House, God

Here is the key to my house, God.
I'm seldom at home
during the day.
Feel free to use it
anytime you need
a place to stay.
Help yourself to whatever
you can find
in the cupboards, refrigerator,
or freezer.
If you need to rest,
lie down on the bed
in the guest room.
Watch TV, listen to music,
read my books and magazines—
why heck, even my journal.

Sit on the deck,
go for a stroll in my garden.
Do whatever you want
or feel like.
The place is yours.

And when I get home
from work,
I'll fix us a bite to eat,
and we'll sit outside
in the back together,
sipping fuzzy navels and
swapping yarns,
until the sun disappears
behind the row
of evergreens.

A few years back, a friend of mine gave me the key to her house, inviting me to use it whenever I felt the need "to get away." I was deeply touched by her openness, generosity, and trust. I remember thinking, "If only I could be that welcoming to God." This poem grew out of that experience. Jesus said, "Come to me, all you who labor and are burdened, and I will give you rest" (Matthew 11:28). Prayer is accepting God's invitation to come away and rest awhile. But prayer can also be inviting God to come into our homes, lives, and hearts.

FOR REFLECTION

1. To whom would you give the key to your house?

2. This poem is about trust and intimacy. How are these qualities in evidence throughout the poem?

Suggested Scripture

Psalm 23   *the good shepherd*

Jeremiah 1:4–10   *the call of Jeremiah*

FOR PRAYER AND PLAY

Rewrite Psalm 23 using other images drawn from real life—for example, the Lord is my grandmother, coach, best friend, gardener, mechanic.

Here We Come, the Church

Here we come
the People of God,
the Church:
kind, cranky,
generous, selfish,
efficient, bungling,
faith-filled, skeptical,
hopeful, despondent,
eager, wary,
broad-minded, short-sighted,
forgiving, vengeful,
alert, asleep,
patient, whining,
magnanimous, petty,
pure, corrupt,
saint, sinner:
here we come,
the People of God,
the Church.

*I*n her book, *Holy the Firm*, the American writer Annie Dillard wrote: "Nothing could more surely convince me of God's unending mercy than the continued existence on earth of the church." The Church continues to exist not because it is perfect, but because its sure foundation is Jesus.

FOR REFLECTION

1. There are many contrasting words in this poem to describe the Church. Can you cite evidence of the validity of some of these words either from history or from your personal experience of the Church?

2. We are the Church, says the maxim. Do you reflect any of the words in this poem in your personal life?

Suggested Scripture

Romans 12:9–12   *mutual love*

Galatians 6:1–10   *life in the early Christian community*

1 Corinthians 1:10–17   *divisions in the early Church*

FOR PRAYER AND PLAY

Read the three descriptions of the early Christian community. List some of the similarities you see between that community and your parish, diocese, or greater contemporary Church. List some of the differences you note. Or, write a paragraph simply summarizing what the Church means to you.

Hope

*Hope is not afraid
to stand out in the rain.
She looks diminishment
square in the eye.
Years ago
she befriended
need and emptiness.
She is on a first-name basis
with darkness, fear, and loss.
She never explains
tears and heartache
away.*

*Hope knows
in Whom her trust lies.*

*She has no need
to stun, overwhelm, or win.
She knows her power
as well as her limitations.
She is very good at waiting.
Best of all,
Hope knows how everything
will turn out in the end.
That's what keeps
her going.*

*H*ope is more than mere optimism. It is rooted in our belief in the life and teachings of Jesus. But it is not a passive virtue. It demands that we work for the world we hope for. Activist Dorothy Day said it well: "No one has a right to sit down and feel hopeless. There's too much work to do."

FOR REFLECTION

1. Why do you think these two lines are set off by themselves: "Hope knows / in Whom her trust lies"?

2. How would you define or describe hope?

Suggested Scripture

Psalm 71:1–8 *prayer for divine help*

Habakkuk 3:17–18 *hope in God*

FOR PRAYER AND PLAY

Think of someone you believe is a hopeful person—either someone you know personally or someone from the news or history. How did they manifest their hope? Or look up some quotations on hope on the internet or in a book of quotations. Are there any quotations you really like? Why?

How Dare Those Yellow Daffodils

How dare those yellow daffodils
bob their perky heads
up and down.
I think I'll put on
big black boots,
go out and stomp them
into the ground.

How dare those little sparrows
chirp and carry twigs.
I have half a mind
to go outside
and rip to shreds
every nest
I can find.

How dare those bees
buzz and flit
from flower to flower—
as if they're sure
there will be a tomorrow.
I'll take a shovel,
and smash their hive
to smithereens.

You died this past winter.
How dare there be
any more springs.

*T*he speaker in this poem is a very angry person. First, she wants to stomp the bobbing daffodils into the ground, rip up all the birds' nests she can find, smash the honey bees' hives to smithereens. We wonder: What has caused such rage toward these signs of spring—a season most of us find delightful? The final two lines reveal the cause: the recent death of a loved one. Grief takes many forms. Anger is one of them.

FOR REFLECTION

1. Have you ever mourned the death of a loved one? What forms did your grief take?

2. Why do you think the speaker is angry at spring?

Suggested Scripture

Mark 16:1–8   *the resurrection of Jesus*

1 Thessalonians 4:13–18   *Christian hope for the dead*

FOR PRAYER AND PLAY

Reflect on some of the losses you have experienced or are experiencing at this time in your life: a loved one, a certain relationship, health, a job, a particular place, one's youth, a change in financial status, etc. At the top of a piece of paper write: To me grief means…. Then finish that sentence in 10 different ways.

I Have Never Seen the Face of God

I have never seen the face of God.
No angel ever came to me.
I have never witnessed a miracle,
a blind man see,
a bent woman stand
straight and tall,
a dead girl sit up and cry,
"I'm hungry."
or 5,000 people fed by two fish
and five loaves of bread.
But I have tasted strawberries,
I have smelled bread baking,
and drunk cool water
and rich, red wine.
I have been lifted up by a
robin's chirp,
and been humbled by the
stars and ocean.
I have planted seeds, pulled weeds,
washed clothes, typed letters,
waited in line, asked questions,
given my opinion, picketed.
I have attended meetings,
read great books, sung in church,
played cards, talked to squirrels,
made repairs, danced the polka.
I have cradled a newborn in my
arms and kept vigil with the dying.
I have fallen exhausted into
bed at night,
and risen again in the morning.
I have said, "I'm sorry...I forgive...
Thank you...I don't know."
I have held someone I love,
and I have been held by
someone who loves me.
I have won and lost,
known sickness and health,
ecstasy and dread.
And through it all,
God is the one who is always present.
God as companion,
stranger, hunger, goad.
God as lover, friend,
tag-along, intruder, foe.
God as answer and as question,
blinding light and dark abyss.
God, God, God.

S ome poems are written in tranquility. This particular one was written amid turmoil and frenzy—which only supports its basic theme.

FOR REFLECTION

1. Which activities in this poem can you identify with? Are there others you would add?

2. Reflect on the descriptions of God in the last five lines. Do any of these descriptions resonate with your experience?

Suggested Scripture

Genesis 18:1–15 *Abraham's visitors*

Psalm 34:1–11 *God delivers the just*

Mark 4:35–41 *the calming of the storm*

FOR PRAYER AND PLAY

After reading the account of Jesus calming the storm, reflect on some of the storms you have experienced during your life. How was God (Jesus) with you during those times? Or read the story of Abraham's visitors. Write a dialogue between Abraham and Sarah in which they decide not to be hospitable to the strangers. What good reasons would they have had?

I'm Over You Now

I'm over you now.
Honest.
I've ripped up your picture,
scratched out your name in my address book,
and given away all the trinkets you ever gave me.
I've gone on with my life.
Honest I have.
If someone asks me how you are,
I say calmly, "I have no idea."
I don't even think about you
anymore.
Honest I don't.

In fact,
I didn't even write this poem.
Someone else did.
Honest.

The speaker in this poem has ended a relationship—in no uncertain terms. Can we believe what the speaker says: "I don't even think about you / anymore"? The final stanza gives us our answer. As the queen says in Shakespeare's *Hamlet*, "The lady doth protest too much, methinks."

FOR REFLECTION

1. Have you ever ended a relationship with someone? If so, how did the end come about—was it mutual, peaceful, stressful, gradual, sudden, easy, difficult?

2. Are there any former relationships you still think about—even though they're over?

Suggested Scripture

Psalm 62:1–9   *trust in God alone*

John 11:1–44   *the death and raising of Lazarus*

FOR PRAYER AND PLAY

This poem describes someone whose actions contradict their words. Write ten sentences that illustrate this human phenomenon—for example, "I hope to lose thirty pounds," she said as she bit into her third jelly donut. Or, "I believe we must love our neighbor," he said as he carefully avoided eye contact with the homeless man sitting on the park bench.

I'm Scared, God

I'm scared, God.
Of what? God asks.
If I knew, I say,
I wouldn't be
this way.
My fear is the gnawing kind:
nameless, shapeless,
more vague foreboding
than certain dread.
What do I do
with apprehension
so nebulous?

Give it to me, God says.
But it's not an "it," I protest.
Then give me yourself.
And so I do.

Entrusting my trembling person
to that all-encompassing embrace,
I hear those words
only Divinity can say
with hard-won certitude:
Everything's going to be okay.
Everything's going to be okay.

*A*s little children, we often ran to our parents when we were afraid. How many times did they comfort us and say these words, "Everything's going to be okay"? God is the Great Comforter—even from those fears we cannot name.

FOR REFLECTION

1. Have you ever felt fear that was of the "gnawing kind" or "nameless, shapeless"? What did you do?

2. What do you think the phrase "hard-won certitude" refers to? Why do you think the last line is repeated?

Suggested Scripture

Psalm 69:1–4; 14–18   *cry to God in distress*

Mark 6:21–43   *Jairus' daughter; woman with the hemorrhage*

FOR PRAYER AND PLAY

Read the account of the woman with the hemorrhage. The gospel says that after she was cured, she "approached Jesus in fear and trembling." What reasons did she have to be afraid? How does Jesus ease her fears? Or, search the gospels for other examples of Jesus' approachability. Then write a prayer to the "Approachable Jesus."

I Saw a Color Today

I saw a color today
with no name.
It wasn't yellow.
It wasn't peach or apricot.
It wasn't off-white, ochre, eggshell,
saffron, mustard, or amber.
And certainly
it wasn't desert sand
or atomic tangerine.
No, it was itself—
uniquely and delightfully so.

And suddenly I knew,
inside of me too
was a color
with no name—
although I think,
on most days,
it's leaning toward
lavender indigo.

I read somewhere that the human eye can differentiate seven million colors. Seven million! I am also fascinated by the creative names paint companies come up with for their wide spectrum of colors—names such as carrot, robin egg blue, lemon chiffon, saddle brown, asparagus, papaya whip, electric purple. But what fascinates me the most is the absolute uniqueness of every human being. This poem combines my love for colors with my appreciation for the uniqueness of individuals—myself included.

FOR REFLECTION

1. What are some of your favorite colors? Why?

2. How has the uniqueness of individuals been a blessing and a challenge for you?

Suggested Scripture

Psalm 139 *ever-present God*

Genesis 1:1–31 *creation story*

1 Corinthians 12:4–11 *variety of gifts*

FOR PRAYER AND PLAY

Write a litany of thanksgiving for the colors of the rainbow. Tell what each color means to you or how it makes you feel. Or give creative names to ten different colors you happen to see today.

It's Up to Me

*This new day
stretches out before me
like a tranquil blue lake.
I can sail across it
or plunge into its depths.
It's up to me.*

*This new day
stretches out before me
like a large, soft blanket.
I can snuggle under it
or picnic on top of it.
It's up to me.*

*This new day
stretches out before me
like a weedless green lawn.*

*I can lie down upon it
or run barefoot through it.
It's up to me.*

*This new day
stretches out before me
like a blank sheet of paper.
I can fill it with words
or paint a picture on it.
It's up to me.*

*This new day
stretches out before me
like a snow-capped mountain.
I can start to climb it
or stand in awe before it.
It's up to me.*

*T*he British writer G.K. Chesterton once wrote, "Here dies another day during which I have had eyes, ears, hands and the great world around me, and tomorrow begins another. Why am I allowed two?" This poem is a reminder of the inestimable value of each new day. At the same time it suggests the privilege and responsibility that is ours to make good use of all the days we are given.

FOR REFLECTION

1. Which image of the new day speaks most to you at this time in my life: lake, blanket, lawn, sheet of paper, or mountain? Why?

2. What are some of the things you can do so you don't take each new day for granted?

Suggested Scripture

Psalm 96 *song of thanksgiving*

Matthew 6:9–15 *Our Father*

FOR PRAYER AND PLAY

If you were told you had only one more month to live, what would you do with those thirty days? Or pray the Our Father slowly and reverently, meditating on each phrase.

It Took Three Men

It took three men
to beat the teenage girl
in the dark blue burqa:
two to hold her down
with her face in the sand,
and one to flog her with a club
across buttocks and legs
as she screamed and pleaded
and struggled to break free.
Her crime?
She was caught alone with a man
who was not a relative.
Afterwards the men explained,
"We were lenient. She deserved
to be stoned to death."

But aren't there worse crimes than hers:
self-righteousness,
absolute certitude,
the lust for control,
not to mention
the morbid obsession
with club and stone?

One day the Scribes and Pharisees brought a woman to Jesus. She had been caught in the act of adultery. "What do you say we should do with her?" they asked Jesus. But Jesus didn't answer their question. Instead he stooped down and began to write something in the sand with his finger. Then Jesus said to them, "Let the one among you who is without sin be the first to throw a stone at her" (John 8:7). And the men all began to walk away. This poem is a contrast to that ancient occurrence in the gospel as well as a commentary on a recent incident I saw on the evening news.

FOR REFLECTION

1. This poem suggests a few reasons why some people judge others harshly. What are they? What other reasons can you think of?

2. Is there evidence that we as individuals, local communities, and nations possess a "morbid obsession with club and stone"?

Suggested Scripture

Psalm 25 *prayer for forgiveness and guidance*
Luke 18:9–14 *parable of the Pharisee and publican*
John 8:1–11 *Jesus and the woman caught in adultery*

FOR PRAYER AND PLAY

Rewrite or retell the parable of the Pharisee and publican set in contemporary times. You might even consider changing the gender of one or both of them. Or, read the account of the woman caught in adultery. After the episode, imagine her telling a good friend about what had happened. What would she say?

Just Because

Here's a poem
I wrote for you,
just because.
It's not your birthday,
you're not sick,
you're not graduating,
you weren't promoted,
you're not about to go away,
and (thankfully)
no one has died.

No,
I wrote this poem for you
just because.

Just because
you are you,
I am me,
and we are we.
That's reason enough
for me.

*D*o we always need a reason to send a card to a friend? Do we always need a reason to get together with our family and loved ones? Do we always need a reason to phone a parent or a son or daughter? This poem answers "no."

FOR REFLECTION

1. What are some of the "reasons" you get together with your friends? Is the friendship alone reason enough?

2. Do you ever send a card to a friend for no reason?

Suggested Scripture

Exodus 33:7–22 *Moses' intimacy with God*

1 Samuel 18:1–5; 20:1–42 *David and Jonathan*

FOR PRAYER AND PLAY

Read the account of Moses' intimacy with God. How is this intimacy revealed? Or read the story of the friendship of David and Jonathan. What words and actions demonstrate their love for each other? Or send a card to a friend for no reason.

Let the Dark Night Come

Let the dark night come.
Let the sun fade behind the distant hill,
Let the wind rise and bring an evening chill.
Let the dark night come.

Let the sparrow retreat to her nest,
Let morning glories turn in and rest.
Let the dark night come.

Let the fox emerge from his lair
Let alien noises fill the air.
Let the dark night come.

Let coyote and badger spy,
Let bat and owl rule the sky.
Let the dark night come.

Let all shadows now hold sway,
Let the blackness have its way,
For God is Lord of both night and day.
Let the dark night come.

*T*oo often we limit God's blessings to the obviously good things in life: friendship, births, anniversaries, healings, successes, kindness, and other good fortune. But then the "dark night" comes, that is, times of pain, failure, death, uncertainty, and we may feel abandoned by God. This poem reiterates the words of the psalmist to God: "Yours the day and yours the night" (Psalm 74:16). It reminds us that life goes on even throughout the night, and God walks with us in the darkness.

FOR REFLECTION

1. Recall some of the "dark nights" you have experienced in your life. How did they make me feel?

2. What helps you to get through these dark nights?

Suggested Scripture

Psalm 91   *security under God's protection*

Luke 22:39–46   *the agony in the garden—Jesus' darkest night*

Luke 23:33–49   *crucifixion of Jesus*

FOR PRAYER AND PLAY

Read one of the passion accounts by candlelight tonight. Or, go outside after dark and look, listen, feel, and smell. What signs of life do you detect even in the darkness?

Life Is Short

Life is short.
Smile.
Life is short.
Play.
Life is short.
Savor.
Life is short.
Pray.

Life is short.
Relax.
Life is short.
Bend.
Life is short.
Wonder.
Life is short.
Befriend.

Life is short.
Apologize.
Life is short.
Dance.
Life is short.
Learn.
Life is short.
Give thanks.

Life is short.
Let go.
Life is short.
Forgive.
Life is short.
Love.
Life is short.
Live.

*R*ecently I read an article entitled, "50 Things to Do before I Die." It encouraged me to draw up a list of specific things I wanted to do before my own death. (Writing a book of poetry was one of them!) "Life is short" is a maxim we hear often. But do we live as if we really believe it?

FOR REFLECTION

1. Which actions listed in the poem do you already do? Which actions do you think you need to do more often in your short life?

2. Are there other actions not listed in the poem that you would add?

Suggested Scripture

Psalm 39:5–9   *the vanity of life*
Sirach 1:1–18   *praise of wisdom*

FOR PRAYER AND PLAY

Draw up a list of twenty things you would like to do before you die.

∽ 28 ∾

Menagerie of Emotions

The way the dog limped,
I knew he was tired
like me.
The way the cat crept under the bed,
I knew she was depressed
like me.
The way the crow squawked,
I knew he was frustrated
like me.
The way the squirrel ran up the tree,
I knew she was afraid
like me.
The way the lion roared in his cage,
I knew he was angry
like me.
The way the owl hooted in the night,
I knew he was lonely
like me.

Often the way I see others,
is really the way I feel me.

*T*he old saying is, "Beauty is in the eye of the beholder." This poem goes further. It says fatigue, anger, fear, and loneliness are in the eye of the beholder too.

FOR REFLECTION

1. Do you ever attribute to others certain states of mind or conditions that you are feeling in yourself? What is the danger in doing this?

2. Jesus was open-minded and a good listener. He really paid attention to people. Can you cite any evidence of this from the gospels?

Suggested Scripture

1 Samuel 16:1–13 *Samuel anoints David*

Luke 5:1–11 *call of Simon the fisherman*

FOR PRAYER AND PLAY

Practice being a good listener today. Give others your attention and time. At the end of the day, take a few minutes to reflect on what you learned about others and yourself by doing this exercise. Or reflect on the way Jesus changed peoples' lives throughout the gospels— for example, Peter, Matthew, the other apostles, Mary Magdalene, Nicodemus, the widow of Naim, Martha, and Mary. How did he influence them so profoundly?

My Mother's Apron

After my mother died,
we divided up
her earthly possessions:
furniture, dishes,
silverware, pots and pans,
exquisite glass bowls from Bohemia.
But one thing I wanted
more than any of these,
was one of her aprons:
blue and yellow print,
with ample bib, long strings,
and two large pockets.
Now every time I put it on,
I, like a priest vesting for Mass,
kiss it tenderly,
begging God for the grace
to serve as humbly
and joyfully
as she did.

I did take one of my mother's aprons after she died. And yes, I do kiss it before I put it on. Her apron is a rich symbol to me of her selfless love.

FOR REFLECTION

1. Do you have any keepsakes from a loved one that you treasure? If so, what are they and why do you treasure them?

2. Look around your house. Are there any items you wish to pass on to loved ones when you're gone?

Suggested Scripture

Matthew 20:20–28   *the request of James and John*

John 13:1–20   *the washing of the feet*

FOR PRAYER AND PLAY

Don an apron today and serve someone humbly and joyfully. Or read the suggested Scripture. What insights into service do these two passages provide for you?

On Seeing Deer

It is a well-known fact:
If you want to see deer,
All your effort and ache
Will not make them appear.
But when you plod, head down,
With mind on lesser things,
And chance a glance: they're there!
Beauty free! Your heart sings!

So, too, Divinity—not
A Presence we secure,
Nor move by pine, nor bid
To show where we revere—
Breaks in as sweet surprise,
Allaying all our fear.
Then our seeing heart cries:
God is here! God is here!

I have lived in several different places where deer routinely roamed. But one thing I noticed: If I went outside in search of deer, they never seemed to show up. It's when my mind was on other things that they would suddenly appear out of nowhere. This experience made me wonder: Does the same principle apply to God? Does God have a way of "showing up" when we least expect it?

FOR REFLECTION

1. Have you ever had the experience of an untamed animal appearing when you least expected it? How did that experience make you feel?

2. Have you ever felt God's presence in an individual or a situation where you didn't expect it? What was that experience like for you?

Suggested Scripture

Job chapters 38—42   *God questions Job*

Luke 18:1–9   *parable of the persistent widow*

FOR PRAYER AND PLAY

Read God's speech to Job. What are some of the ways God reminds Job of his lowly humanity? The speech raises the issue of how little control we humans have over our existence. Reflect on Job's response to God at the end of this section. What is he really saying? Can you put it into your own words? Or read the parable of the persistent widow. What does this parable say to you about prayer?

Otters

Otters, they say,
nuzzle smooth stones for hours
for no other reason than pure feel.
In winter,
they belly down slippery slopes
not to get from here to there,
but solely for the ride.
And when they sleep,
otters intertwine with other otters—
brothers, sisters, spouses, kids—
all in one warm furry heap.

Yes, otters work.
They fish,
defend their territory,
and teach their young to forage,
but only for a fraction of their day.
Otters (unlike most of us)
save their best
for play.

*O*tters are lucky. Their food supply is usually abundant and readily available. This leaves them considerable free time for other things—such as play. We can learn a lot from animals. This poem raises the question: how do I allot my time?

FOR REFLECTION

1. How does this poem capture the daily life of otters?

2. How good are you at balancing work and responsibilities with leisure and play in your life?

Suggested Scripture

> Psalm 98   *sing to God*
>
> Matthew 7:25–34   *dependence on God*

FOR PRAYER AND PLAY

Today do something fun you really enjoy doing. Or keep track in writing this week of all the times you played. Or reflect on what other animals can teach us about living.

Please Grant Me This One Morsel, God

Please grant me this one morsel, God.
Like the Syrophoenician woman,
I do not ask for banquet fare,
but merely for a table scrap.

On every given day I pray,
"Thy will be done."
But today I beg Thee for this
one
small
crumb.

*T*he Syrophoenician woman had great spunk. She was daring for even approaching Jesus, since she was Greek and not Jewish. It also took courage for her to beg Jesus to cure her daughter. But when Jesus hesitates and even seems to insult her, she is not deterred. Her witty comeback wins over even the Son of God.

FOR REFLECTION

1. Is it okay to ask God for little things—a sunny day, a parking space, help on a test, another small favor? Why or why not?

2. Do you ask God for things? If so, what kinds of things? If not, why not?

Suggested Scripture

Psalm 88:1–10   *prayer in time of distress*

Mark 7:24–30   *the Syrophoenician woman*

FOR PRAYER AND PLAY

Read the account of the Syrophoenician woman. Suppose later she was arrested for being a follower of Jesus. You are the prosecuting attorney. What evidence of her guilt would you present based essentially on her encounter with Jesus? Or, compose seven petitions that could be used at your parish on a typical Sunday.

A Poem Is Something You Let Out

A poem isn't something you write down,
it's something you let out.
It needn't be very long,
but just the size it has to be.
A poem doesn't require fancy phrases,
just a few good words
and a few good spaces.
A poem needn't tell all there is to tell,
but just one thing, and one thing well.
A poem doesn't have to
scream, weep, or shock.
It only has to say,
then stop.

*M*any poets have written about poetry. Robert Frost said, "Poetry is when an emotion has found its thought and the thought has found its words." Gwendolyn Brooks wrote, "Poetry is life distilled," while Carl Sandburg penned, "Poetry is a packsack of invisible keepsakes." To the words of those great poets, I humbly add my little poem about poetry.

FOR REFLECTION

1. What are your thoughts and feelings regarding poetry?

2. What do you think of the quotations by the three poets above?

Suggested Scripture

Ecclesiastes 3:1–8   *an appointed time for everything*

Psalm 131   *humble trust in God*

FOR PRAYER AND PLAY

Write your own poem about poetry. Or read a poem or two by your favorite poet(s) today.

Prayer Is a Cinch

Prayer is a cinch.
All you do
is cut a three inch
incision
below the navel
and let some of your guts
spill out;
or
lie on your back
on the ground,
arms at your side,
mouth open wide,
and let
God
give you
CPR;

or
go stand on a hill
during an electrical storm
and wait to be struck
by lightning;
or
hitch a ride on a rocket
to the North Star
and try to enjoy
the journey
of 100,000 years.

*P*rayer is a paradox. Who can really define or describe it? At times it can be a great joy, but at other times, pure torture. Prayer can take myriad forms too, as this poem illustrates. The only essential ingredients in prayer seem to be God and me, or God and us.

FOR REFLECTION

1. Do any of the images of prayer in this poem speak to you? If so, why? If not, why not?

2. How would you define or describe prayer?

Suggested Scripture

Mark 1:32–39 *Jesus heals and prays*

John 17:1–26 *Jesus' prayer at the Last Supper*

Matthew 26:36–46 *the agony in the garden*

FOR PRAYER AND PLAY

Read the three Scripture accounts of Jesus praying that are listed above. What do these three passages reveal to you about prayer? Or write your own poem entitled "Prayer Is…."

Prayer of the Tuckered Out

O God, look down upon me,
So weary, worn, and stooped,
And hear the humble prayer
Of one who's really pooped.

I ask not for good fortune,
Nor for serenity.
Instead one thing I beg you for:
How 'bout some energy.

Sometimes I'm not so good, God,
I fight, complain, and shout.

I offer no excuses,
Except I'm tuckered out.

My spirit is so willing
It wants to do what's best,
The problem is my flesh, God,
for all it wants is rest.

This prayer should be much longer,
but what else can I pray when
I'm too dog-tired to stay awake?
Have pity, God. Amen.

I have read many books on prayer. One of the best pieces of advice I ever came across were these words by Dom Chapman: "Pray as you can and do not pray as you can't. Take yourself as you find yourself; start from that." Getting sufficient rest is foundational for not only our physical and psychological well being, but also for our spiritual health.

FOR REFLECTION

1. Take an inventory of your prayer life today, reflecting on these questions: How do you ordinarily pray? Where do you prefer to pray? How do you begin? What do you do during prayer? How do you conclude? Do you use any aids for prayer?

2. Are you getting sufficient rest to support a healthy spiritual life? If so, how do you do it? If not, what can you do about it?

Suggested Scripture

Mark 6:30–32 *apostles go away with Jesus to rest*

1 John 4:16b–21 *God is love*

FOR PRAYER AND PLAY

Recall some advice you have been given about prayer, or look up some quotations on prayer—either in a book or online. Which advice or quotations do you like the most? Why? Or interview a few people (in person, on the phone, or online) about their thoughts on prayer.

Road Kill

Let's say you're driving down the road
and up ahead you see a furry creature
on the side of the road,
getting set to run across from left to right,
and so you slow down and plan to veer left,
figuring the thing will run straight across the road
and you will miss it
—but you are wrong—
for just when you get near to him or her—
(it's a squirrel, you can see that clearly now)—
he or she stops dead in its tracks
in the middle of the road
and then darts left again
right under the tires of your car
—thump, thump—
and you squirm in your seat
and utter a mild profanity
and are tempted to glance
in the rear view mirror
to see for sure
if you hit him or her,
I tell you:
DO NOT LOOK INTO THAT REARVIEW MIRROR.

Figure it this way: If you didn't hit it
(that's another thing: always think of it
as an it. Forget that he/she, him/her business)
and the thump, thump was indeed only a bump in the road
then the thing is already safely back
on the left side of the road
and halfway up a tree by now.
And if you did hit the stupid thing
(yes, it WAS a stupid thing,
a stupid, stupid thing
for not running straight across the road
like anything with half a brain would do)
then you do NOT want to see
what the rearview mirror might show.
TRUST ME ON THIS:
With road kill,
(as with other unfortunate mistakes in life),
the thump thump is bad enough,
but the sight of the writhing and the final twitch
could haunt you
forever.

This poem is about more than hitting a poor squirrel in the road. It is about other "unfortunate mistakes" we make throughout our life. It raises these questions: When should we recall our past mistakes (that is, look in the rearview mirror) and when should we forget them?

FOR REFLECTION

1. This poem races along. How does the structure support the content and theme?

2. Are there any "unfortunate mistakes" in your past that you dwell on? Are there some that you should forget? What makes the difference?

Suggested Scripture

Psalm 51 *prayer of repentance*

2 Samuel 11:1—12:25 *David's sin and repentance*

FOR PRAYER AND PLAY

On a sheet of paper write some of your mistakes, failings, bad habits, or sins. Fold the paper and read prayerfully Psalm 51. Then shred, tear up, or burn the paper. Or read the story of David's sin and repentance. Despite his grave sin, what good qualities does David display in these chapters?

37

Saving the World

Jesus did not leave behind
a three-ring spiral notebook
labeled: How to Save the World.
He did not leave behind
a file cabinet stuffed with
folders marked
Faith, Hope, Love,
Recruiting Strategies,
Financial Planning,
and Pro-active Public Relations.
He did not leave behind
his journal,
his password or his Blackberry.
Instead,
Jesus left behind
the gentle sway of who he was;
his integrity, compassion,

prayerfulness,
longsuffering, and forgiveness.
He left behind
the bread and wine
of his life and teachings,
and his total surrender
to a terrible death
borne of unselfish love.
He left behind
a handful of followers,
radically made new
just by his presence.

We will save the world
in only one way:
by being transformed
into his beautiful person.

I am always amazed at how little we leave behind when we die—some money perhaps, a few pictures, an heirloom or two. But often the greatest gift we bequeath to others is the memory of who we were and the "gentle sway" of our love. When Jesus died he left behind one earthly possession: his seamless tunic. Yet here we are 2,000 years later still being transformed by his presence.

FOR REFLECTION

1. What are some of the ways individuals or groups have tried unsuccessfully to save the world? Why didn't these ways work?

2. In what ways are you being transformed by the "gentle sway" of Jesus' "beautiful person"?

Suggested Scripture

John 19:23–25   *the soldiers and Jesus' tunic*

Philippians 2:5–11   *Jesus emptied himself*

FOR PRAYER AND PLAY

The novel (movie) *The Robe* focuses on what happened to Jesus' robe after his death. Read a synopsis of the story or write your own imaginary account of what happened. Or list the qualities Jesus possessed or the teachings of his that have influenced your life the most.

38

She Recognized Him

"Jesus said to her, Mary!" JOHN 20:16

She recognized him
in the way
he spoke her name.
How was that?
With tenderness?
eagerness? joy?
impatience?
or simply
a certain intonation
that was uniquely
his?

As for me,
how do I recognize
his call?
What name does he choose,
what intonation does he use
to say:
I am uniquely
his?

$\mathcal{A}$ few months after my brother John died, I awoke one morning to the sound of his voice calling my name. I didn't actually hear it with my ears, but I did hear it clearly and distinctly in my heart. Just my name. Nothing else. And pronounced in the subtle but unique way that only he said my name. The experience was immensely consoling for me.

FOR REFLECTION

1. List all the names you have—from formal names, more informal names, nicknames, names at work, names from childhood. Who calls you by these various names? Do you like hearing your name pronounced by certain individuals more than others? If so, by whom and why?

2. What name(s) does God call you? What name(s) do you use to address God in prayer?

Suggested Scripture

Genesis 2:18–20   *Adam names the animals*

John 20:11–18   *Jesus' appearance to Mary Magdalene*

FOR PRAYER AND PLAY

Read the story of Jesus' appearance to Mary Magdalene. Circle the verbs in the account and reflect on their significance. Or, pretend you are Adam, and God has given you the task and privilege of naming the animals. Choose about a dozen animals and give them new names. What did you learn about yourself from doing this exercise?

She's Always Five Minutes Late

She's always five minutes late.
Always. And always five.
Not seven. Not four and a half.
But five. On the dot.
How does she do it? I wonder.
How can she be so
punctually unpunctual
All the time?
Do all the clocks in her house
run exactly five minutes slow?
Or was she born
five minutes late
And she's been playing
catch up ever since?
And what does she do with
all those five minuteses
She's had to enjoy while
we're forced
To waste all of ours
Waiting, waiting, waiting
For her to show up?

I picture her snuggling extra
in bed,
Sipping one more cup
of coffee,
Calling and laughing
with a friend,
Dusting the top
of her refrigerator,
Arranging her photos in
neat little albums.

I suspect
When the angel of Death
Comes to take her away,
She'll say,
"I'll be with you
in a minute, Dear,"
and be five minutes late
for eternity.

*M*y mother was never late for anything. In fact, she was usually several minutes early for everything—doctor's appointments, Sunday Mass, wedding receptions. As a result, I grew up to be a very punctual person. Little wonder then that unpunctual people frustrate me. So I took out some of my frustration (good naturedly, I hope) by writing this little poem.

FOR REFLECTION

1. Do you tend to be punctual or unpunctual? Does it really matter if you're late or early for things?

2. What are some of your "pet peeves"—those small annoyances that frustrate you? How do you deal with them?

Suggested Scripture

Acts 2:42–47   *the early Christian community*

1 John 4:7–16a   *Christian love and life*

FOR PRAYER AND PLAY

Read the description of the early Christian community. Do you think it is too idealistic? Why or why not? Then write a description of your parish, diocese, religious congregation, prayer group, or the Church—at its best. Or after reading John's description of Christian love, write your own description.

Sometimes Everything Works

Sometimes everything works,
the light goes on,
the car starts,
the joint is pain free.
Sometimes plans go well,
the tree blossoms
the dough rises,
the project is a success.
Sometimes people are good,
they offer to help,
they say "I'm sorry,"
they mend their erring ways.

Sometimes hard work pays off,
the cure is found,
the mystery is solved,
the catastrophe is avoided.

Sometimes.

But it's mainly
during those other times
we discover
what we're made of.

*T*he old proverb says, "It's easy to hold the helm when the sea is calm." Similarly it's easy to be a believer when everything is going our way. But what happens when we encounter the vicissitudes of life? Can we still be a faith-filled person? Can we still have hope?

FOR REFLECTION

1. This poem lists examples of things going well. Can you name some other examples you experience in life?

2. In your mind, rewrite this poem changing the happenings to negative experiences: for example, "The tree dies, the dough falls flat." What are some of the negative experiences that have challenged your faith?

Suggested Scripture

Psalm 70   *prayer for divine help*

2 Corinthians 11:16–33   *Paul's labors and suffering*

FOR PRAYER AND PLAY

On a sheet of paper, make two columns. Head one "things that went well." Head the other "things that did not go well." Then list incidents in your life under each heading. What did you learn from this exercise? Or, read about Paul's labors and sufferings. How have you worked because of your Christian faith? Have you ever had to suffer because of your faith?

Speak, Lord

Speak, Lord,
your servant is listening.
Should I do this
or that
or something else
altogether?
When?
Where?
How?
Could you please be
more clear?
Could you give me
a map or blueprints perhaps,
or (better yet)
how about a script
complete with stage directions?

Your servant is listening,
Lord. Speak.
And please, please
enunciate.

Sometimes we find ourselves saying, "I will do whatever God says. But right now, I don't know what God wants me to do." Discerning "God's will" is not always easy. Sometimes, God does seem to mumble! But at such times we must recall that God rarely spoke directly to individuals—even the greatest saints. Often God spoke indirectly through circumstances, events, inner stirrings, and other people. God is not in the habit of providing us with "a script/complete with stage directions." But, in another sense, we do have a map and blueprints. How about Scripture? How about the life and teachings of Jesus? How about a good person we love and can trust?

FOR REFLECTION

1. What are some of the ways you discern the will of God for your life?

2. What are some Scripture passages or stories that you have used to direct your decisions and choices?

Suggested Scripture

1 Samuel 3:1–18   *the revelation of Samuel*

Jeremiah 20:7–9   *Jeremiah's interior crisis*

FOR PRAYER AND PLAY

List ten ways God speaks to you (through a particular individual, some aspect of nature, a certain Scripture passage, etc.). Listen to one of these ways very carefully today.

മ 42 ൌ

Speed

I worshiped speed.
How fast
can I go?
How soon
can I get there?
How much
can I accomplish
in just one hour?
But today
I stopped to let a turtle cross the road,
in quest of a mate, perhaps,
or a safe place to lay her eggs,
and I thought:
she's getting
somewhere too:
steady, determined,
sure.

And I concluded:
speed matters less
than direction, intent,
and perseverance.

*S*ome of us are speedaholics? We do everything at a rapid pace—whether eating our lunch, driving our car, talking to people, or even praying. Delays annoy us. We hate to wait—for anything. This poem suggests that we consider slowing down a bit. After all, the things that make life worth living—community, family, friendship—all demand time.

FOR REFLECTION

1. To what extent are you a speedaholic or not? Prove it.

2. Why do community, family, and friendship demand time?

Suggested Scripture

Psalm 104   *praise of God as creator*

1 Corinthians 13:1–13   *St. Paul's hymn of love*

FOR PRAYER AND PLAY

Read St. Paul's hymn of love slowly and prayerfully. Can you think of some individuals who have largely lived up to these words? saints? other historical figures? someone you know personally? someone you've read about or seen on the news? To what extent have you lived up to these words? Or, if you are a speedaholic, deliberately slow down for a day. How did you feel at the end of the day?

Standing on the Stage of Life

Standing on the stage of life,
we play our part
as best we can,
some days bringing down the house,
other times eliciting only boos.
But always
God is there,
standing in the wings,
prompting us,
urging us on,
and clapping enthusiastically
even when,
beyond the footlights,
silence reigns.
God,
our indispensable audience
of one.

*I*n the letter to the Romans we read: "If God is for us, who can be against us?" Good question. If we truly believe in God's special and unconditional love for us, then what or whom have we to fear? The nearness of God is one of the great themes in Scripture.

FOR REFLECTION

1. Have you ever experienced the "applause" of others? What was that experience like for you? Have you ever experienced the "boos" of others? What was that like for you?

2. When does God feel far away for you? When does God feel near?

Suggested Scripture

Psalm 118:5–14   *song of thanksgiving*

Romans 8:28–39   *God's great love in Jesus*

FOR PRAYER AND PLAY

This poem uses the image of God as a prompter in the wings of a stage. What are some other images you can come up with for this loving and encouraging God? Or write your own hymn of thanksgiving similar to Psalm 118.

Surely He Danced at Cana

"I should only believe in a God who would know how to dance." FRIEDRICH NIETZSCHE

Surely he danced at Cana.
After all,
it was a wedding feast.
And it was the custom
for men and women
to dance,
only in those days,
in separate groups.
I can see him now,
hands above his head,
feet stomping,
body swaying,

head thrown back,
singing a song
he loved and knew by heart.

When we hear of the
miracle at Cana,
we think of his changing
water into wine.
But let us not forget
that other miracle:
he showed us a God
who loves to dance.

*T*he gospels don't tell us everything Jesus did while he walked our earth. But some things we can deduce by knowing the geography of the place or the customs of the times. Chances are, Jesus walked a lot and spent a lot of time outdoors. Chances are he sang too. And chances are, he danced.

FOR REFLECTION

1. Is it easy or difficult for you to picture Jesus dancing? Why or why not? Does it make any difference whether he danced or not?

2. What role does dance play in your life? in our worship?

Suggested Scripture

Exodus 15:19–21 *Miriam and the other women dance*

2 Samuel 6:14–23 *David dances before the ark*

Psalm 149 *praise God in festive dance*

John 2:1–11 *the wedding at Cana*

FOR PRAYER AND PLAY

Read Psalm 149 and the accounts of Miriam and David dancing before God. What is the connection between faith and dance? Or dance for God today.

Taking for Granted

He said,
"I read somewhere
that over 50% of all marriages
end in divorce.
And malaria's on the rise again
and so is crime and the
infant mortality rate.
There's more corruption
in politics
than you can imagine.
And did you know
water pollution
is far worse than we thought?
And don't get me started
on all the cheating in sports,
the bacteria in our food supply,
and the perilous condition
of our nuclear power plants."

After I left him
I went home,
kissed my wife,
played ball with the kids
and later
took the dog for a long walk
beneath the stars,
giving thanks to God
for all that was right
in the world,
and for all I was taking
for granted.

*I*t's a fact: most of the news we read about in our newspapers and see each day on TV is bad news. That's not to blame the news media. For it's been proven that bad news simply sells better than good news. But if our picture of the world is only what we get from the news media, we will end up with a skewed view of reality. Yes, there are awful things happening in our world. And yes, we should be aware of them so we can take measures to address them. But there are a lot of good things happening in our world too—things not always reported by the news media, things right under our very noses.

FOR REFLECTION

1. What is some of the "bad news" being reported by the news media today? Is there some "good news" being reported by the news media?

2. What "good news" is part of your personal life right now?

Suggested Scripture

Psalm 92 *thanksgiving to God*

1 Corinthians 1:4–9 *Paul's thanksgiving for the Corinthians*

FOR PRAYER AND PLAY

Write your own psalm of thanksgiving, modeled on Psalm 92. Thank God for specific peoples, places, things, and events in your life. Or scan the news for some "bad news," and turn your reading into prayer and action.

A Teacher's Lament

Other kids would sit up tall,
they'd listen and obey.
They'd give their full attention,
to every word I say.

Other kids would get along,
they'd follow my directions,
They'd do their work with eagerness
and always ask good questions.

Other kids would be polite,
they'd smile at me a lot.
But I don't teach those other kids,
I teach the ones I've got!

*A*ll teachers dream of teaching the perfect class. But the reality is, there is no such thing as perfect students. Some students are lazy or bored, others are hostile or arrogant. No one has the perfect teaching environment either. Teachers suffer from small classrooms, inadequate equipment, distractions of all kinds, and the human imperfections found throughout the school community. But the truth is, even Jesus the Master Teacher didn't have ideal students or ideal teaching conditions. He worked with the individuals he had. His love for them helped him to deal with their imperfections.

FOR REFLECTION

1. What are some of the problems and annoyances in your world right now from which you would like to escape? Are you ever temped to wish for an ideal world?

2. Someone has said, "Reality is God's home address." What does that mean to you?

Suggested Scripture

Psalm 86:1–7 *prayer in distress*

Matthew 18:1–5 *the greatest in the kingdom*

Mark 10:13–16 *Jesus and little children*

FOR PRAYER AND PLAY

Reflect on Jesus' words in Matthew 18:1–5. What qualities do children have that make them good candidates for the kingdom? Or play with a little child today and thank God for children.

There's a Little Voice Inside My Head

There's a little voice inside my head
who always puts me down.

When someone says,
"You're so warm and welcoming."
The little voice says,
It's just your genes.

"Your presentation was excellent."
Not everyone thought so.

"You're a good writer."
Others are far better.

"You've helped me so much!"
That was God's doing.
Not yours.

"You cooked a great meal!"
You got lucky.

"You're such a good friend."
You forget birthdays.

I tell myself
I will muffle
that voice
once and for all
and not heed it again.
But then I hear:
You don't have the guts
to do that.

Some of us are our own worst enemies. We are constantly putting ourselves down. If someone pays us a compliment, for example, rather than simply saying, "Thank you," we downplay or even deny the person's words. The little voice inside our heads is persistent. At least, that's been my experience.

FOR REFLECTION

1. Have you ever heard a little voice inside your head saying negative things about yourself? If so, what does it say? How do you deal with it?

2. What are some ways you can be a positive "little voice" for others?

Suggested Scripture

Psalm 57 *prayer for deliverance*

John 13:31–35 *the new commandment*

FOR PRAYER AND PLAY

Write a dialogue with your little voice similar to this poem. Then re-write it, answering each negative response your little voice has said. Or write an encouraging note to someone who's struggling today.

ᴄᴏ **48** ᴏᴠ

They Left Me for Dead

They left me for dead
on the side of the road,
a bleeding pulp of a man.
Then he came by—a Samaritan.
I wanted to tell him,
"You're too late, Buddy.
They took it all."
But I could form no words
with my broken jaw.
Then I felt his touch—
so gentle—
and then the oil and wine
he poured over my open wounds.
And I closed my eyes,
and yielded myself
completely
to his tenderness.

The innkeeper tells me
he brought me here
on his own donkey
and nursed me through the night.
He's gone now,
but he said he'd be back
in a day or two
to check up on me.

All the while those thugs
were beating me,
I kept asking,
"Why? Why? Why?"
But this Samaritan—
all he's done for me—
How can this be?
How can this be?

M. Scott Peck, author of the best seller *The Road Less Traveled*, was a therapist for many years. He said, during those years his clients often asked, "Why is there so much evil in the world?" During those same years, not one client ever asked, "Why is there so much good in the world?" This poem is built on that theme.

FOR REFLECTION

1. Have you ever asked, "Why is there so much evil in the world?" Have you ever asked, "Why is there so much good in the world?"

2. Who has ministered to you in your need? To whom have you ministered?

Suggested Scripture

Psalm 142 *prayer in time of trouble*

Luke 10:29–37 *parable of the Good Samaritan*

FOR PRAYER AND PLAY

Pretend you are the man who was beaten up by robbers and cared for by the Samaritan. You are being interviewed by a TV reporter. She asks, "How has this entire experience changed you?" How would you respond? Or pretend you are the Samaritan. The reporter asks you, "What made you do what you did?" What do you say?

They Tore Down My Old School Today

They tore down my old school today—
James A. Garfield Elementary School—
right before my eyes.
I had stopped by to see it
for one last time
before bulldozer and wrecking ball
were unleashed against
red brick and white pillar.
Standing at a safe distance,
I watched in horror
as a dinosauric steamshovel
lumbered toward the building,
lurched forward and took a huge bite
out of Miss Enniert's third grade classroom.
GARRRRUNCH!

Walls crumbled, dust flew everywhere.
I could almost hear Miss Enniert inside
saying to us calmly and even cheerfully,
"Now boys and girls, crawl under your desks
and curl up into a little ball.
Everything's going to be okay."
She always knew what to say and do
for every kind of looming disaster:
fire, tornado, atomic bomb.

But I sense
even Miss Enniert,
(God rest her soul)
would have stood mute and powerless
as I did today,
against the relentless encroachment of Change,
the steady demolition of Time.

*W*hen I got the word that my old school was about to be torn down, I grabbed my camera (and my sister) and rushed to take a few pictures of it before it was razed. I snapped pictures while the demolition crew did its heart-wrenching work. Within a short time, the entire structure was leveled. The razing of my elementary school led me to reflect on other "levelers" we experience in life such as illness, natural disasters, wars, and death itself.

FOR REFLECTION

1. What remembrances do you have of the schools of your childhood? Are they essentially positive or negative? Do you remember any teachers in particular?

2. What is your basic attitude toward change? Do you find it easy or difficult? Why?

Suggested Scripture

Matthew 5:1–12   *the Beatitudes—a major change in attitude*

Acts 11:1–18   *a significant change in the early Church*

FOR PRAYER AND PLAY

Take a sheet of paper and divide it into two columns. Head the first one "changes I liked." Head the second one, "Changes that were hard for me." Try to come up with 10 changes (large or small) for each column. Did you learn anything about yourself by doing this? Or write a letter to Death.

⚬ **50** ⚭

This Vale of Tears

It is a vale of tears at times
this earthly life.
A place of cold and darkness,
fear and pain,
where smiles take leave,
songs are silenced,
and dance becomes impossible.
A place of no clear vision,
no solutions, no way out.
A place where nothing
makes sense anymore.
Nothing.

And so we huddle together,
reciting the words in hushed tones
and telling the stories again,
while waiting,
waiting, waiting—
for what, we do not know—
desperately clinging
to what we still have:
each other
and his promises.

*T*he "Hail, Holy Queen" is a beautiful ancient prayer to Mary in which we say, "To you do we send up our sighs, mourning and weeping in this vale of tears." Sometimes our earthly pilgrimage can be filled with beauty and joy, but at other times we definitely walk in a "vale of tears."

FOR REFLECTION

1. What do you think these phrases mean: "reciting the words…retelling the stories…his promises"?

2. Reflect on a time when you felt you were walking in a vale of tears. What was it like for you? How did you get through it?

Suggested Scripture

Psalm 13   *prayer during time of distress*

John 20:19–29   *Jesus appears to the disciples*

Acts 2:1–13   *Pentecost*

FOR PRAYER AND PLAY

Recite the "Hail, Holy Queen" prayerfully, meditating on each phrase. Or read a newspaper or watch the news and pray for those individuals who are walking through a vale of tears today.

Today Was a Very Good Day

Today was a very good day.
In fact, it was a wonderful,
enchanting, remarkable,
amazing, marvelous,
miraculous, tremendous,
stupendous, glorious,
awesome day.

What's more,
nothing
out of the ordinary
happened.

*W*hat constitutes "a very good day"? A dream is fulfilled? A major goal is accomplished? Something extraordinary happens? A miracle occurs? This poem gives a different answer. It celebrates the miracle of every day.

FOR REFLECTION

1. When you say, "I had a very good day," what do you usually mean?

2. What determines whether something is ordinary or extraordinary? Can something be both at the same time? Explain.

Suggested Scripture

Daniel 3:57–88   *Let all creatures praise the Lord*

1 John 1:1–4   *the Word of Life*

FOR PRAYER AND PLAY

Go through the adjectives used in this poem. For each one, name one person, place, thing, or event that that particular adjective could describe for you. Come up with other positive adjectives of your own and continue your reflection.

The Toll of War

I heard this
from a young woman
who was actually there
when the war burst
into her small town.
Guns roared,
bombs rained down,
corpses were strewn
in the vacant streets.

"And all the birds left," she said.

I tried to fathom
a chirpless, wingless place,
and to comprehend
the toll of war
on other things
besides ourselves:
birds, bees, trees,
rocks, rivers, butterflies—
who tallies
their demise?

*A*fter every war, there is usually a grisly accounting of the casualties: the dead, the wounded, the missing in action. But this poem reminds us that we have never really measured the complete toll of war on planet earth.

FOR REFLECTION

1. What has been your experience of war—through personal experience, the news, books, movies?

2. What are some of the other "casualties" of war besides those listed in the poem?

Suggested Scripture

Psalm 72   *king of peace*

Isaiah 11:6–9   *the peaceable kingdom*

Luke 24:36–43   *Jesus' appearance after the resurrection*

FOR PRAYER AND PLAY

Read prayerfully Psalm 72, a psalm that describes a king of justice and peace. Are there any phrases or lines in this psalm that remind you of Jesus? Or go online or find a book or magazine that speaks of peace. Can you take anything it says and apply it to your own personal life? Or have a conversation with someone who has been in war. Listen well.

To My Mother

As the paramedics
were wheeling you
out the door
that morning,
the oxygen mask
clamped firmly
over your nose and mouth,
you suddenly motioned
for them to stop,
and for me to come closer,
as if you had
something urgent
to say.
And I,
bending over you,
with tears in my eyes,
ready to catch
what could be
your final words
to me,
heard you gasp:
"Unplug
the coffee pot!"

*W*hen a friend of mine described this incident with her mother, I knew there was a poem there. Her mother (like my own) was a very practical person. And yes, though she was having an aneurism that morning, she had presence of mind to remember a small detail of daily living. I am happy to report that she did miraculously pull through and lived for several more years. This poem is a tribute to all strong and practical people who play a crucial role in keeping death (in its various forms) at bay.

FOR REFLECTION

1. Define or describe what "being practical" means to you. What's good about being practical? Can there be any liabilities connected with being practical?

2. What would you like your last words to be?

Suggested Scripture

Proverbs 31:10–31 *the good wife and mother*

Luke 10:38–42 *Mary and Martha*

FOR PRAYER AND PLAY

Read the account of the good wife and mother in Proverbs. Does it remind you of any women you have known in your lifetime? Reflect on some of the women who have made a deep impact on your life. Compose a litany of thanksgiving for them, listing the gifts each one gave you. Or read the story of Mary and Martha. Which woman do you most resemble? Prove it.

Two Little Sparrows

Outside my bedroom window
on the roof of the porch
two little sparrows were doing it.
He had trouble with balance at first.
Luckily, she was the epitome of patience.
The whole affair lasted but a moment.
And when they were through,
I clapped.

Why?
Simply because
two little sparrows
got together
to make new sparrows,
despite the toil of care,
potential storms,
droughts, cats,
and circling hawks everywhere.

I am constantly amazed by the tenacity of life: a green shoot springing up in a crack in the sidewalk, a purple crocus pushing up through the snow, a little chick pecking a hole in its shell. I am even more amazed by the courage and strength of individuals I have known who persevere despite great setbacks, succeed despite terrible odds, and retain hope despite gloom and disaster. This poem is a tribute to them.

FOR REFLECTION

1. What are the obstacles these two little sparrows have to face in their lives? What similar obstacles are we humans apt to face?

2. What enables individuals to persevere despite setbacks, succeed despite terrible odds, and retain hope despite gloom?

Suggested Scripture

Psalm 27   *trust in God*

Ruth   *the entire story*

FOR PRAYER AND PLAY

Scan the newspaper or internet for stories of individuals who have faced serious hardships and yet remain people of joy and hope. To what do they attribute their ability to do this? Or, after reading the book of Ruth, write a letter that Naomi might have written to a friend after the marriage of Ruth and Boaz.

55

The Way You Just Looked at Me

The way you just looked at me
when we met by chance on the street—
as if coming upon Niagara for the very first time,
or finding at last the right word for the puzzle,
or catching the scent of fresh bread in the oven,
or spotting, from your deserted island, the top of a sail,
or coming in shivering and beholding the fire—
for that way,
all I can say is
thank you,
my friend.

*T*he British writer, C.S. Lewis, wrote: "Friendship has been by far the chief source of my happiness." Friends are individuals who make us feel welcome, accepted, and loved. They do this in countless big and little ways—sometimes simply by the way they look at us.

FOR REFLECTION

1. Has anyone ever looked at you in the way this poem describes? If so, how did it make you feel?

2. Have you ever looked at a friend in the way this poem describes? Why?

Suggested Scripture

Ecclesiastes 4:9–10 *two are better than one*

Sirach 6:14–17 *friendship*

Matthew 18:20 *where two or three are gathered*

FOR PRAYER AND PLAY

Make a list of qualities that you think are essential for friendship. To what extent do you find these qualities in your best friends? in yourself? Or write a thank you to a friend for their friendship with you.

56

What's New?

Every time
I'd visit Mom
in the nursing home,
she'd say, "Hi, Honey!
What's new?"
And I'd scrounge around
for things to share with her.
Sometimes,
coming up empty,
I'd say, "Nothing's new, Mom.
Just the same old stuff."

Shortly after she died,
I planted a kiss
on her still warm forehead,
trying to fathom
what she was
experiencing now—
luminous light?
longed-for reunion?
the dissolution of all pain?—
and I whispered in her ear:
"Hey, Mom,
What's new?"

*I*n his first letter to the Corinthians, St. Paul writes, "No eye has seen, nor ear heard, nor the human heart conceived, what God has prepared for those who love him" (1 Corinthians 2:9). We can only begin to imagine what heaven will be like—based on the "heavenly experiences" we have here on earth. For me, the love of my mother is one of those experiences.

FOR REFLECTION

1. What experiences here on earth are foretastes of heaven for you?

2. Why is it important to keep in mind that our earthly life is not the whole of life?

Suggested Scripture

Psalm 8 *God's majesty and human dignity*

2 Corinthians 5:1–10 *our future destiny*

FOR PRAYER AND PLAY

You have been asked to explain heaven to a small child. What would you say? Or, reflect on these three phrases from the poem: "luminous light, longed-for reunion, the dissolution of all pain." What do those mean for you? What other phrases might you add?

While the Goose Just Sits

I wake up, get dressed,
make breakfast,
check the newspaper,
pack lunches,
kiss my husband,
get the kids off to school,
while the goose just sits
on her nest.

I drive to work,
check my email,
speak to my boss,
answer the phone,
fill out a report,
run a meeting,
while the goose just sits.

I form a committee,
draw up a plan,
solve a problem,
run to the bank,
call my mother,
type a letter,
while the goose just sits.

I pick up some milk,
take the kids to practice,
throw a load in the washer,
fix some supper,
eat with my family,
walk the dog,
while the goose just sits.

I help my son with homework,
dry the tears of my daughter,
fold the clothes,
water the flowers,
nestle with my husband,
go to sleep for the night
while the goose just sits.

There are many kinds
of devotion,
from perfect stillness to
endless motion.

I have always admired how birds (like geese and chickens) can sit for weeks on their eggs to get them to hatch. During that entire time they do basically nothing except sit, sit, sit. What devotion! Yet is the young mother running hither and yon for the sake of her family any less devoted than the brooding goose? I think not. Hence, this poem.

FOR REFLECTION

1. What does devotion mean to you? What are some forms you have seen it take?

2. Is busyness good or bad? Explain.

Suggested Scripture

Song of Songs 8:6–7   *true love*

Matthew 23:37–39   *Jesus' lament over Jerusalem*

FOR PRAYER AND PLAY

Keep track of what you do for a day. Jot these activities down. Which ones give evidence of your devotion to someone or something beyond yourself? Or go on line or get a book of quotations and read some quotations on love, noting which ones you definitely agree with and why.

SUGGESTED
SCRIPTURE REFERENCES

(the number refers to the number of the poem)

INDEX OF
THEMES AND TOPICS

(the number refers to the number of the poem)